Karin Walker established KGW Family Law in Woking, Surrey in 2012. She is a mediator, arbitrator (finance and children) and a collaborative practitioner. With co-trainer Suzanne Kingston she has provided innovative family law training online since 'lockdown' in March 2020 and together they have trained mediators in the specialised form of mediation known as 'hybrid'. She is also a co-founder of 'The Certainty Project' with Julian Bremner and Margaret Kelly, a new way of working in family law which combines mediation and arbitration and provides the couple with certainty of duration and cost, hence the name.

Karin is recognised by both the Legal 500 and Chambers and Partners as a leader in her field. She regularly writes articles on a number of topics associated with family law and has appeared in the media locally and nationally. Karin also speaks locally, nationally and internationally on all aspects of family law.

Having been a member of Resolution (formerly the Solicitors Family Law Association) since admission as a solicitor, Karin was an elected member to Resolution's National Committee for two terms (resigning in 2017) and Chair of the National DR Committee from 2014 to 2017. In 2016 Karin became a member of the Worshipful Company of Arbitrators and a Freeman of the City of London. In 2020 she became a Liveryman.

A Practical Guide to Divorce for the 'Silver Separators'

A Practical Guide to Divorce for the 'Silver Separators'

Karin Walker
KGW Family Law
Solicitor, Mediator, Arbitrator and Collaborative Practitioner

Law Brief Publishing

Published 2020 by Law Brief Publishing, an imprint of Law Brief Publishing Ltd
30 The Parks
Minehead
Somerset
TA24 8BT

www.lawbriefpublishing.com

Paperback: 978-1-913715-42-7

To my husband John and our two children,

Stefanie and Tristan

PREFACE

As the marriage rate falls and the majority of 'millennials' choose to cohabit, the over 60s top the divorce charts. There are several reasons for this growing trend.

Couples who married in the 1970s often did so at a relatively young age. Cohabitation was less socially acceptable at that time and therefore marriage, particularly for those in their late teens and early 20s, was commonplace.

As the average life expectancy increases, those who are now reaching retirement age see themselves as having twenty-five to thirty years ahead of them. The sedentary lifestyle associated with retirement is no longer attractive.

Individuals change radically during adult years and often in different directions, resulting in a level of incompatibility which was not prevalent at the time of marriage. Life expectations and values change along with interests and social interaction.

All of these factors compound to cause separation to become likely.

Very often one party is the protagonist, the other being more content with the traditional move towards retirement.

As a consequence, the 'silver separators' are fast becoming the most likely age group to consider divorce.

For reasons which will be explored, the 'silver separators' have very specific issues which require resolution on separation, meaning that those advising them need an understanding of, and ability to deal with, those issues to construct, or advise on, a satisfactory outcome, taking account of future requirements.

So why do I have an interest in this topic? I have found that, certainly in the last five years, the clients whom I represent over the age of 55 are growing in number and forming an increasingly substantial section of my practice. In addition, as people live longer, they are finding themselves wanting to separate at a much later stage in their lives and indeed couples are now separating even in their 80s and 90s. The specific group who are the focus of this handbook are broadly between the ages of 60 and 75.

Why is this demographic of client so unique that it warrants special consideration? What is it about this group of people which makes them require a slightly different level of understanding and approach from the lawyers who represent them?

The emotional fall out after a long marriage is inevitably more extreme and more likely to have a demonstrable and lasting effect on either or both of the couple, even if in different ways.

Pensions and future income derived from pension will have a significant impact alongside general income issues post retirement. Division of pension on divorce is sadly a growing area of negligence claims for family practitioners and a clear understanding of the potential pitfalls and how these can be covered is therefore essential.

Either or both of the couple are likely to have received an inheritance of some description and there may be a need to 'unravel' inherited wealth.

One of the couple (or even both) may have a new partner who may be younger and may have their own children. This can add to the emotional and financial complications and the uncertainty of the future.

The law referred to in this book is correct as at 21st September 2020.

Karin Walker
September 2020

CONTENTS

CHAPTER ONE
HOW TO DEAL WITH THE EMOTIONAL FALLOUT AFTER A LONG MARRIAGE

When any couple separates it is unusual for both to be in agreement that the relationship has broken down and it is time to move on in different directions. More often this is a decision taken by one of the couple which the other then has to try to come to terms with emotionally.

Where the couple have been together for a long time (in excess of 25 years and often over 40 years) this is even more of an issue. The couple may have been in a relationship together for practically all of their adult life. It is entirely likely that one may have been the breadwinner and the other the homemaker with the latter being entirely reliant on the former for financial arrangements and security. The fear of having to face the later years of life alone and emotionally unsupported (even if that 'support' were more limited than perhaps was appreciated) can be frightening and utterly beyond comprehension.

Particular emotional issues for the 'silver separators' are as follows:-

- The couple are each in a completely different place. One is looking at new horizons and a change in lifestyle whereas the other is focussing on retirement/grandchildren etc.

- The difficulties experienced by adult children when their parents separate including the potential loss of a 'home base'.

- One of the couple may have had no involvement at all in the family finances and need to re-educate or rely on professional advice.

- Expectations with regard to future standard of living and how this should be provided.

- Will one or both of the couple work beyond retirement age and what effect does this have.

- The impact of a new partner and a new family.

- Possible health issues.

The 'silver separators' will most likely have married at an early age, probably because living together was not an option for them. They may have married for reasons which were unlikely to ultimately stand the test of time. They may not have become fully developed adults at the time of their marriage and their desires and objectives may not have been aligned. The arrival of children and financial constraints may have 'glued' them together, sometimes for decades. Compromise may have become the 'least worst' option with the couple running their lives often in parallel and sometimes in separate 'bubbles' with each occupying an independent world either at work or at home, joining together in the evenings, at the weekend and during the holidays.

For those couples who married because it seemed like the 'right' thing to do when they were very young and did not have many other options if they wanted to be in a relationship, compromise and acceptance of a situation is something which they will more often than not have embraced for a very long time.

In this age group, perhaps more than any other situation, the decision to separate is driven by one of the couple. These people will have more than likely changed and developed in very different ways over the period of a long marriage. As people move towards retirement age some become determined to rid themselves of a dissatisfaction which may have burdened them for some time. With children having moved into adulthood, perhaps with their own families, and retirement meaning the start of the final third of one's life rather than being the 'wind down' to the end this is the time for a re-evaluation and perhaps change.

More often than not however this is a decision which is taken by only one of the couple, usually the one who's working life has taken them away from home during the week and who therefore has been exposed to a different and ever changing way of life to the other. The other member of the couple may have become embedded in the community of the family home location and see the future as providing support to children and grandchildren and adopting a more leisurely way of life as a couple.

The discovery that your life partner, to whom you may have been married for in excess of 40 years, wants to bring the marriage to an end and move in an entirely different direction can be devastating and even emotionally disabling. The communication of such a decision can in itself have a major effect. Adult children, for reasons which will be expanded upon, often take their parents separation very badly as it can rock the very essence of their own security and stability even if they no longer live at home. The result can be an emotional 'car crash'.

If you are acting for the protagonist of the relationship breakdown you need to explain to them at the outset that initially they will have to give their spouse time to catch up with their decision which they may find difficult or even impossible to comprehend. Although your client may have agonised over what they should do for some time before taking legal advice, when they do arrange to take that advice they will have made the decision and want to get on and implement it, not least because they may feel that time is not on their side. They may not be in a place to consider or comprehend the impact which that decision will have on their wife/husband.

How that decision will be communicated is something to which careful consideration must be given. This is something which may not have taken place when you first meet with your client. Probably you may want to have a draft letter agreed to go out from your firm before any discussion between the couple takes place. You need to show empathically but firmly that the relationship is over and try to steer the couple towards resolution of short and long term financial and other arrangements. This is not least because the system lends itself to delay and undoubtedly your client, now that they have decided what they want at this stage in their life will want to 'get on with it', They do however owe it to their spouse to warn them 'face to face' that they will be receiving a letter from their solicitor advising that they want to bring the marriage to an end.

Do bear in mind that, very infrequently, your clients will be cohab-itees, living under the misapprehension that there is such a thing as a 'common law wife' and probably in a situation where all property (and possibly all resources) will be in the sole name of the husband. I have suggested that this age group tended to marry young because living together was not so acceptable, but very occasionally they will have opted for that arrangement. Where the children are adult so that no Schedule 1 claim under the Children Act is an option, the task of telling the spouse who owns nothing that they may be asked to leave with no capital, pension share or financial support of any kind, can be an invidious one. It is a severe but short conversation and of course the lawyer is likely to have limited further contact with their client whichever of the couple may have contacted them. If you are acting for the financially disadvantaged spouse do not have any misconception of how this information which they almost certainly did not suspect is likely to affect them and have to hand the details of other professionals from a more therapeutic background who can provide much needed on-going help and support.

Putting cohabitees to one side, I am alluding to the fact that it may, more often than not, be the husband who has decided that he wants life to be different to that which might have been expected and has decided to take the plunge and move in a different direction in a way that has permanent repercussions.

It is however perfectly possible that the protagonist for the divorce might be approaching the situation from a wholly different direction. The mind-set of this age group is quite likely to result in the establishment of a parallel life with one of the couple having an affair (or even multiple affairs) and initially the other nor realising or turning a blind eye but then eventually deciding that they will not put up with this any longer and have decided to take action. The emotional 'fallout' in the case of this scenario can be even greater. The person having the affair may want their 'cake and eat it' and may have absolutely no wish for their marriage to come to an end with all the financial implications which that will mean. The spouse who has decided 'enough is enough' may have reached that decision unwillingly, being encouraged by friends, family or even adult children, and be taking steps which deep down they would prefer not to have to take at all.

So from the point of view of the family lawyer it will be extremely important at the outset to understand exactly what the position is from the point of your client; how emotionally able they are to give proper instructions; what sort of additional professional support might be of benefit to them and how that might be provided and whether a tactical approach to the process might be just as important as providing sound and pragmatic legal advice.

Be very wary of the client who wants to be accompanied by one of the adult children to the first meeting with you. Try to work out the motivation for this approach and, if possible, suggest someone else stressing the importance for children of any age not to have to take 'sides'.

Initial meetings with new clients in this age bracket can take longer than usual. In most cases on party will not want to divorce. Whichever of the couple is your client, this is something which you will have to take on board and work with. Even if your client appears to be taking the initiative they may be doing so very reluctantly.

Do also be conscious of the prevalence of what is described as 'narcissistic personality disorder' and other personality disorders in this age group which could have a major impact upon you as a legal advisor. This area is a whole separate topic but it is important to be cognisant of the possibilities and how/if you might cope with them.

Whatever the facts of the particular case might be, separating couples in this age group will be shrouded in an emotional situation which will require more than just your legal knowledge and skill to navigate toward a successful outcome for your client.

We shall look in turn at the particular issues which will almost certainly arise.

CHAPTER TWO
PENSION ISSUES FOR THE 'SILVER SEPARATORS'

The failure to provide proper information and deal appropriately with the issues surrounding pension sharing on divorce is probably the principal growth area for successful negligence claims in family law. Scarily there are now organisations to whom you can take your Court Order and pension sharing annex(es) and they will evaluate for you (for a fee) whether you might have a negligence claim against the lawyer who represented you as a consequence.

There are plenty of books written about pension sharing arrangements; the purpose here is to indicate what should 'raise alarm bells' for you and, most importantly underline the need for independent advice.

The report of the Pensions Advisory Group dated July 2019 is a 'must read', probably for all family practitioners but definitely for those acting on behalf of clients who fall into this age bracket. This was the outcome of two years' work undertaken by a group of experts from a diverse background in this field. To be honest, practitioners are now faced with the choice of reading and implementing the guidance provided by the report or running the risk of being negligent.

The report looks at the main definitions and concepts of pensions on divorce and there is a comprehensive glossary at appendix A.

The essential stages when dealing with pensions on divorce are set out in the report as follows:

- *Gathering of information in relation to all pensions, including state pensions*
- *Careful review of whether any of the 'complicating factors' may be present (there are 26 listed in the report)*
- *Review of the valuation figures and whether they are reliable and reasonable*
- *Service of applications on the pension fund trustees*
- *Consideration of whether an expert report is needed*
- *Finalising the approach to, and particulars of, valuation and division of pension assets*
- *Completion of key court forms*
- *Seeking pension administrator approval*
- *Consideration of when to apply for Decree Absolute*
- *Implementation*

The PAG have provided a 14-page executive summary to the report itself which summarises the key points. Although this provides an excellent overview, it is not a substitute for reading the report itself.

At Appendix E you will find an extremely useful draft letter of joint instruction to a PODE (Pensions Expert On Divorce).

The report also comments that form D81 provides insufficient information in relation to pensions and requires updating and that section 2.13 of Form E does not ask sufficiently clear questions to obtain all relevant information. Watch out for changes in these forms!

As the report says, '*ignoring the pensions or agreeing to ignore the pensions is not an option*'. Without doubt, the same could be said of the report itself.

As a basic 'rule of thumb' if the couple (or at least one of them) are over the age of 40 with pensions which have a CEV of £100k or more then you should have a pension sharing report. Clearly it would be surprising if there were not a pension sharing report in every 'Silver Separators' case.

Particular issues for parties over the age of 60 are:-

- One of the couple may hold the majority (if not all) of the pension provision – and consider it to be 'theirs'. This could include a final salary scheme.

- There may have been insufficient pension contributions made during the marriage to support the couple living together during retirement, never mind living separately in two homes which require funding.

- One of the couple may have made pension contributions which pre-date the marriage nd believe that these should be 'ring-fenced'.

- Insufficient state pension contributions may have been made by the party who did not work. This is something which should always be considered at the commencement of the case – and is often overlooked

- Exceeding the threshold for lifetime pension contributions and the tax implications. The allowance for 2020/2021 (state pension being excluded) is £1073,100.00

- A desire to 'offset'.

In a 'silver separator' case it is frequently the case that one party has been the 'breadwinner' during the marriage with the other not having worked at all or having sporadic, often part-time, forms of employment. It is not unusual for the 'breadwinner' to view their pension as belonging exclusively to them.

It is useful to remember that pension sharing came into effect on 1st December 2000. Where a divorce petition was issued prior to that date pensions would be retained by the person in whose name they were held with no alteration to the other assets as a consequence. Those who were in practice at that time will doubtless remember the surge of husbands desiring to issue divorce proceedings before the deadline!

A 'silver separator' is likely to have been aged around 40 in 2000 and would undoubtedly have had friends or family who were engaged in the divorce process for whom pension sharing would have been irrelevant. It is easy to understand how one might erroneously believe that pension sharing only takes place where there are pensions on both sides and that otherwise the pension is retained by the person who has worked for it. Dissuading a client of that misconception can often be difficult, particularly if it is the pension holder who is the driving force behind the separation and their calculation of future income has been based on having the full pension income at their disposal. This can come as a real shock.

At the initial meeting with a 'silver separator' husband (particularly if he is the one who wants to bring the marriage to an end) this is a point which you will need to raise and clarify. Income arrangements in retirement can be a major issue for clients in this category. If in fact your income moving forwards will be 50% less than that which you anticipated, it can even cause you to re-evaluate any potential decisions about the future.

You may find yourself acting on behalf of the wife with the husband unrepresented in this situation. You will need to have a strategy in place to explain the need for a PODE to provide a report and the fact that some form of pension sharing order is an inevitability.

Income deficit is a real problem for couples separating in later life. The automatic enrolment started for workplace pensions only in 2012 and unless one of the couple has the benefit of a final salary scheme pension contributions may not have been a priority expenditure in earlier life, particularly if school fees were being paid. The earlier generation benefited from huge house price increases in the 1960's and 1970's which supplied surplus capital when downs-izing. The 'silver separators' of today do not have the same luxury and are potentially facing a sharp decrease in standard of living in the event of separation unless there is a different or ongoing source of income.

Unhelpfully, section 25 of the Matrimonial Causes Act 1973 refers to 'standard of living' being a relevant factor to be taken into account on separation. Clients are quick to assume that this means that their standard of living while married is to continue in the event of divorce. What is actually means is that the 'bracket' of standard of living will be taken into account, i.e. a family living on an income of £50k per annum will have a different level of reasonably incurred expenditure to the family living on £100k per annum and so on. The concept can be very difficult to comprehend, although reality testing will quickly demonstrate that two homes cannot be supported to the same standard ongoing by the same level of income as one home was supported in the past.

Employing the services of an IFA to look at the available assets and income alongside accommodation and other capital needs and a lifetime expenditure budget can be an extremely useful resource. If the couple are on reasonable terms this might be by way of a joint instruction, perhaps alongside the mediation process. If the situation is more acrimonious it is a step which could be taken individually. Reality can be harsh and a clear understanding of what can be achieved financially from the assets and income which are available can be important information to gather at an early stage.

Of course, the obligation on both parties to maximise income is not time limited and if needs simply cannot be met the only alternatives are an injection of additional income if achievable or a down grading of expectations.

The situation can be aggravated if one of the parties has a new younger partner with a reasonable or even high level of earned or other income which will provide that household with a far higher standard of living. This is something which will be expanded upon later.

It is extremely likely that a pension sharing report will be required when acting for clients who fall into this age bracket. It is vitally important to give careful consideration to the drafting of the letter of joint instruction to the PODE. Each calculation requested will give rise to increased cost for the report so think about why you are asking for a calculation at a particular age .The PAG report suggests that the standard retirement age plus the date when the largest available pension can first be drawn are the most sensible dates.

Of course, a pension may already be in payment. Or you may be looking to disregard pre marriage contributions. What is certain is that a 'one size fits all' draft letter would be inappropriate and in fact probably quite dangerous and that each case should be carefully considered on an individual basis.

For the 'silver separators' the available pension resources will form the basis of future income for at least one of the couple so this is an area which requires the most careful consideration, not least because reliance on pension income will either be immediate or imminent.

In many cases the desire on the part of one of the couple (usually the wife) to retain the family home may be high. If the other party has a new partner who already has a home this can be attractive if it means the retention of all or most of their pension as a result of 'offset'. A solicitor should not advise on the quantum appropriate for offset without expert advice from a PODE. This is the biggest area of negligence risk. That which may seem initially attractive for both of the couple may not be in the long-term best interests of either or both of them.

As a family lawyer it is important to bear in mind that we are not pension experts and to recognise when we need external expert advice. Since 2000 pension sharing has been an important element of financial remedies on separation but this is particularly true when the couple are nearing, or one or both have reached, retirement age. Knowing what you cannot be expected to know and who to ask is essential.

The PAG report makes it clear that asking a client to simply sign a disclaimer if they do not want to spend the money on a pension sharing report is not sufficient. Remember that if it is the wife who would like to retain the family home and she is also the weaker financial party it may be easy for the other side to persuade her into an undesirable offset arrangement and that the cost of a report from a PODE is an unnecessary expense. As their lawyer you need to be able to demonstrate that you have taken all possible steps to carefully explain why a report is desirable and most probably vital and that to sidestep such expert guidance can be disastrous on a short and long-term basis.

Of course, you cannot force a client to do something they do not wish to do but the onus lies with you to demonstrate that a decision **not** to have a report follows you making strenuous effort which are clearly documented to provide advice to the contrary. This is an area where the obligation to be meticulously careful cannot be overstated.

When looking at the pension issues it may also be necessary to consider whether it would be financially preferable for the couple to remain married from a pension perspective with the value not being shared and the widow/widower's entitlement being retained. You may want to consider the benefits of a Deed of Separation or Judicial Separation petition.

CHAPTER THREE
ADULT CHILDREN AND THE EXTENDED FAMILY

Where you are acting for the 'silver separators' their adult children may quickly become one of the very difficult and complicated aspects of the case.

Whereas young children tend to be less impacted by the separation of their parents than the parents would like to believe and as long as they see both their parents and everything else in life is reasonably stable they are ok, this is very often not the case when the children are already over the age of eighteen. The potential issues are numerous and can have a major impact.

A. The child who 'takes sides' and wants to support one of the couple

For all kinds of reasons one or both of the couple may be accompanied to the first (and other) meeting with the solicitor by one (or more) of the adult children. At first they will maintain that they are providing support (and that may be true). You will need to try to work out exactly what their agenda might be and how beneficial (or not) their involvement might be.

When a long marriage comes to an end and one party decides to leave, particularly if the other is more vulnerable both emotionally and financially the children may rally round. Whilst, certainly initially, support of any kind can be of enormous benefit, the children are for the most part the wrong people to provide it. Their presence and involvement can often place their parent under undue pressure and make it very difficult for them to form long term outcomes.

When an adult child learns of their parents' impending separation this can give rise to very mixed emotions and concern about the following:-

- Where one parent has formed a new relationship, a perceived need to support the other parent.
- A feeling that their family base (even if they no longer live at a home) will no longer be there for them.
- A concern about future inheritance upon which they may have (unconsciously) relied for the future.
- A concern that they may find themselves looking after/supporting a parent unexpectedly.

Particularly where one parent has formed a new relationship it is not unusual for one or more of the children to provide support for the parent whom they perceive to be "abandoned". This can often drive a "rift" between family members. On occasion, siblings will form different views which can lead to further hostility and acrimony.

Whilst this support is (perhaps) provided for the best of reasons, it is always advisable to be wary of the situation where your client is accompanied to a first (or other) client meeting by an adult child and even more so when the client authorises you to discuss with/take instructions from that adult child.

Adult children have a feeling of 'injustice', particularly where one parent has left the other or intends to do so. Inevitably they also have their own financial agenda. Often parents may have provided or earmarked funds for house deposits etc. Where a divorce situation emerges such generosity often can no longer be sustained which can cause numerous problems, particularly where an older sibling has already been financially assisted.

Where you have an adult child who wishes to take control of the situation on behalf of their parent (whom they may perceive to be vulnerable and perhaps financially inept) it is vitally important to ensure that the instructions provided accord with that which is in the best interests of the parent rather than the child.

It is also important to remember that children, even when adults, continue to have two parents and a need to have a meaningful ongoing relationship with both. Whilst a child arrangements plan can be implemented to ensure that this ongoing relationship is maintained for a minor child, there is no similar facility for adult children. It can often be important for the instructed solicitor to endeavour to separate out that which might be much needed emotional and general support from self-interest and a level of involvement which can be damaging not only to your client but to the family as a whole. This will be expanded in the case study.

B. The child whose predominant concern is a loss of financial support from their parents

As the cost of living becomes increasingly expensive it is not unusual for 'children' to remain living at home well into their 20's and even 30's. It is also not unusual for parents to provide financial support in the form of a house deposit and even income supplement.

When a divorce situation arises the needs of the couple are the only relevant needs to be dealt with in the context of financial remedy proceedings (unless the couple are in agreement that they should continue to provide a level of financial support jointly to their children). This can mean that funds which were earmarked to provide a house deposit etc. must now be utilised to meet the income and capital requirements of the parties to the marriage.

Such situation can cause a difficulty between the couple. The spouse who has instigated the separation may take the view that it is no longer possible for adult children to be provided for at quite the same level as has historically been the case. It may indeed be one of the reasons for the breakdown in the marriage. The other parent may expect indications of future financial support to be honoured, particularly where an older child has already received this benefit.

Largely as a consequence of the emotional impact on an adult child of their parents' situation, an emotional and unrealistic reaction can often be the end result, accompanied by a level of unrealistic expectation on the part of the adult child.

This can add an additional layer of complication for the couple. Not only do they need to deal with their own financial arrangements but they are also having to attend to the feelings of disappointment and resentment even which may emerge from their family. This can be particularly difficult when their respective approaches to this are different. It is a situation which needs to be identified at an early stage in the process (ideally at an initial consultation meeting) and the solicitor needs to have a plan in place as to how this can be resolved without it having an undesirable level of impact on the overall financial remedy situation, particularly as adult children have no ongoing entitlement to financial support from their parents.

It is a situation where a family consultant may be of benefit.

C. One parent is leaving the marriage to commence a relationship with a new partner who has their own children

The introduction of stepchildren can often present difficulties, but this is particularly the case where one of the parents leaves the other for a younger partner who has children much younger than those of the couple in question. There is the obvious risk of resentment where a parent may be providing a home, an income, perhaps school fees for the children of their new partner in preference to providing financial support (perhaps historically promised) to their own children. That parent may be persuaded by their new partner that in fact their own (adult) children have had financial support during their minority (perhaps in the form of school fees or other financial provision) and that they should now be at a stage where they are self-supporting.

The likelihood of tension between the “abandoned” spouse and the new partner is high. The existence of a new “family” who may well be requiring financial support will add to the already acrimonious and potentially hostile situation.

Again, at a first meeting, it is vital to ascertain from your client exactly who is involved in this situation and the detail of their extended families. Emotional reactions will be one of the main impediments to resolving matters time and cost efficiently and therefore having an understanding at an early stage as to who may be involved is vital.

The acquisition of a new family will also have an impact on future inheritance.

D. The child who is concerned by a potential loss of inheritance

Whether consciously or not, it is not unusual to make an assumption that at some point in the future one's parents will die and that some form of inheritance will be forthcoming. This can cause potential difficulties, even in circumstances where families remain intact.

Where parents separate later in life however, their own financial requirements are likely to change. The arrival of a new partner will alter the position on inheritance, particularly if the parent remarries. Either parent (but usually the father) may have a second nature family. The acquisition of stepchildren, however, is even more likely.

Emotional bonds and a potential level of dependency while in minority are both likely to develop and have an impact on the "first family".

Sadly, human nature is such that financial changes can often bring out the worst in everyone involved. Adult children who had an expectation of a level of inheritance, which is suddenly likely to change can have a very adverse impact both on the child/children themselves and their approach to the relationship of their parents.

It can be very useful to draw a family tree and to identify as the lawyer involved, exactly what the relationship is between all of the extended parties involved in the case. An idea of everyone's age is also helpful. This will enable you to advise your own client on not only their own needs and entitlements, but also their obligations to others (including their children) and what the acquisition of future obligations might cause by way of impact.

Ideally, you do not want any "surprises" to pop up further down the line and, therefore, an understanding of the complete picture and family dynamic at an early stage in the process is invaluable.

Young children often cope far better with the separation of their parents far better than the adults involved expect them to do. This is because they are of an age to be adaptable and as long as they have sound attachments already in place they will soon get used to their new way of live which operates between two homes.

Adult children however have a far more difficult set of circumstances to cope with. Even if they have left home long ago and now have their own home and family they may still regard the home of their parents (which may also have been their childhood home) to be their base and stability. They may still have their childhood memories stored there. Adult children also often retain a bedroom at their parents' home regardless of age. The loss of this can have a major impact at any age.

What can be even more difficult is the situation of the 'adult' child who has not yet left home but is perhaps at university. Where there is insufficient capital to purchase two substantial homes the provision of ongoing accommodation for such adult children may not be financially achievable and they may find themselves with no home to return to at the conclusion of tertiary education or a need to move out of home as a young adult before they expected to do so as the provision of accommodation for them is not a financial consideration for the court. This can cause friction and difficulty for the family as a whole and a feeling of resentment for the parent perceived to be the cause of the marriage breakdown.

This can have a very adverse impact on the resolution of financial matters and create significant tension which will need to be managed as far as possible by the lawyers involved. The long-term effects for the family as a whole should not be underestimated.

Adult children are often being supported financially by their parents in addition to the provision of (often rent free) accommodation at home. Where there is no entitlement to the provision of ongoing support the parent with whom the children continue to permanently reside may find themselves financially compromised as they continue to provide support but perhaps without any assistance from the other parent who is either unwilling or unable to help out. This again can be a source of friction.

The alternative is that the financially stronger parent will provide for the children in a way which the other parent can't, again causing resentment and distorting the family dynamic in a way which undermines stability.

The law remains arguably unfair when considering the needs ongoing of children over the age of 18 who may not be financially independent in reality but are legally expected to be so. They are either thrown into self-sufficiency on a 'sink or swim' basis or the way in which they are helped out (or not) becomes a source of acrimony and unresolvable dispute between their parents. It is a factor which is extremely difficult to deal with if the parents hold differing views but must not be ignored as an emotional and potential financial factor for the separating couple. Harsh and sometimes highly unpalatable advice may have to be given and the consequential effect will need to be evaluated even if nothing tangible can be done.

Parents all too often assume that their adult children can 'cope' with their separation when in reality this can be very far from the truth. The lawyers involved will need to carefully discuss the potential issues with their clients in order to raise their awareness and try to pre-empt any of the issues detailed above which may arise.

CHAPTER FOUR
INHERITANCE ISSUES FOR THE 'SILVER SEPARATORS'

Inheritance or inherited wealth can cause difficulties for 'silver separators' from two different perspectives:-

a) Almost certainly by their stage in life they will have inherited from their own parents or other relatives. This inherited resource may be have been "intermingled" into the family finances, perhaps forming part of the purchase price of the family home or funding improvements thereto; perhaps meeting the cost of school fees or expensive holidays and other luxury items such as new cars. Alternatively, the inherited resource may have been 'ring fenced' perhaps in the form of a property held in the sole name of one spouse or an investment portfolio.

b) The couple will be looking to regulate their own affairs and deal with their own inheritance planning. These arrangements may be turned upside down as a consequence of their separation.

Dealing first of all with wealth which has been inherited, subject to the needs of either of the couple that which has been 'ring fenced' may be capable of retention. That which has been "intermingled" may, however, form part of the joint resources and therefore be available for immediate division.

There is an important difference between funds which have been put into the family home, either as part of the purchase price, a future reduction of any mortgage, or as payment of the cost of improvement or extension. The value of the family home is likely to be divided equally between the couple (unless 'need' should dictate otherwise) whereas inherited wealth which has been kept separate and apart from the joint resources may be capable of being ring-fenced unless required to meet 'need'. Where there is an expectation that inheritance can be simply recovered this can be an area where misunderstandings and possible resentment can arise.

In addition, one of the couple may not yet have inherited but may have parents or other relatives who could face the cost of residential or other healthcare rendering their estate quite limited at the point of death, although this requirement may be uncertain. This can cause friction if the spouse who has already inherited feels that they are having to share their inheritance, whereas the spouse who has the good fortune to have their parents still living has the potential for future capital. After a long marriage, this perceived imbalance can be seen as unfair.

Once again, the first meeting with the client is so vitally important. The need to gather extensive information at an early stage impacts on so many areas which will be potential issues for this couple separating in later life. Essential questions relate to whether or not inheritances have already been received by either or both of the couple, and the purpose to which this resource to which the couple have not jointly contributed has been put. What are the potential sources future inheritance and for whom?

It is also necessary to ascertain whether any trusts are in place, either from which the couple might benefit, or which they have put in place to benefit their own family. Has anything been put in place to defeat the claims of the other spouse under the guides of providing for the family, when in reality one of the couple simply plans to move resources away from the potential claim of the other.

Particularly where you are considering the possibility of out of court methods to resolve ongoing financial and other issues, a very clear understanding of the total picture at an early stage is essential.

It is also important to identify the potential problematic areas and to give consideration to whether additional third parties support might be required, perhaps in the form of a family coach or consultant.

In every divorce situation the lawyers involved will advise upon the need to make a new Will. With the "silver separators", this will go a stage further. They may have engaged in inheritance tax planning, which perhaps can no longer proceed. They may need to revisit the plans which they had for their own family, and the way in which they propose to distribute wealth to the next generation. Separation may cause them to have very different standpoints on these issues which hitherto had been in unison.

The law of England and Wales imposes no obligation to make financial provision for adult independent children on death. It is not unusual however for children to have an expectation of inheritance and even to base their own financial arrangements, even unconsciously, upon such expectation. The arrival of a (younger) new partner or spouse and a second family (step or half siblings) can have a dramatic effect on future financial provision. A property jointly owned will pass on death to the surviving joint owner, not under the terms of the deceased's Will, often creating an unexpected outcome.

Where one of the couple has a new partner but children from a previous relationship and a former spouse with an ongoing level of dependence as a result of spousal maintenance, very careful consideration should be given to the terms of a future Will, ideally to negate the need for any Inheritance Act claims and to ensure that on death assets are distributed in a way which accords with the testator's wishes and expectations. It is not unusual for inaccurate assumptions to be made. It is important to balance the entitlement of a dependent former spouse with the needs of a new partner and subsequent family.

As already outlined, potential loss of inheritance can be a major issue for the children of the Silver Separators and a driving factor behind the stance which they take and the involvement which they have in the event of their parents' divorce. This can also have a regrettable and unattractive effect upon the relationship between the separating couple's children and a second family.

A divorce lawyer will need to

- Find out as much about the background at an early stage

- Talk to their client about what provision they may wish to make for dependents and other members of their extended family.

- Make sure that inaccurate assumptions about inheritance are not being made.

- Be aware of the impact of choices made by your client on their spouse and also the wider family and how this might affect the case generally.

- What similar steps might be taken by the lawyer on the other side.

- Consider the need to sever the joint tenancy on any jointly owned properties in contemplation of divorce.

- Think about what life insurance may already be in place or could be taken out to ease an otherwise potentially difficult situation.

- Be aware of the need to ask questions in order to illicit important information which might not be automatically provided by our client or considered relevant in the first instance.

- Always update this information as circumstances may change.

- Be prepared to have difficult conversations both with your client and also the lawyer acting for the other spouse.

It may be sensible to involve a colleague from your firm's private client team at an early stage or, if you are a niche family practice, to have formed close links with private client practitioners who can assist as part of a team.

CHAPTER FIVE
THE DEATH OF EITHER PARTY PRIOR TO THE CONCLUSION OF DIVORCE PROCEEDINGS

When one is acting on behalf of a client who is in the later years of life the possibility of the death of either of the couple is a situation which could arise prior to the completion of the divorce or financial remedy proceedings.

In every divorce situation consideration must be given to whether or not the severance of any joint tenancy might be appropriate. Whereas some years ago this is something which may have been done as a matter of course, one does need to give consideration in each individual case as to whether this is appropriate. In some circumstances it may be beneficial to your client to continue to be the joint owner and as a consequence of which the surviving joint owner in the event of the untimely death of their spouse. This may particularly be the case where the death of either party is only likely through accident or misadventure.

Where the parties are in the later years of their lives specific consideration should be given at the outset to whether it is desirable for any joint tenancy to be severed, thereby enabling the client to make a will in contemplation of divorce or after pronouncement of Decree Absolute which ensures that their share of any jointly owned property will pass in accordance with their wishes under the terms of their estate.

If either party were to die before the granting of the Decree Absolute and before the finances have been formally resolved, the surviving spouse will still be a dependent for the purposes of inheritance, no matter how long the parties have been separated. Ensuring that a will is prepared in contemplation of divorce may therefore be an essential consideration.

Where one party dies during the pendency of the divorce action, meaning a final Decree Absolute of divorce has not been issued by the Court, the divorce proceeding stops and is withdrawn. The couple remains married and the status of the survivor is that of widow or widower.

Similarly, the division of matrimonial property will cease. The widow/widower will benefit under the terms of any pension provision on that basis.

Very careful consideration needs to be given where financial arrangements have been implemented in part. A binding agreement which is clearly contractual would need to be honoured. Otherwise, however, the resources would pass either under the terms of the deceased's will or under the Intestacy Rules.

This is another situation where the involvement of children can become an issue, as very often they are likely to be the beneficiaries of the deceased parents' estate if a will has been made.

Consider a situation where, by agreement, the family home has been solved and one of the couple has received a proportion of the net proceeds of sale to enable them to purchase independent accommodation which is purchased in their sole name. The family home was held in joint names. The balance of the proceeds of sale are held to the joint order of the couple by one party's solicitor, pending resolution either by agreement or adjudication. The totality of the remaining proceeds of sale would pass to the surviving spouse in the event of the death of the other, as those sums form the residue of a jointly owned resource.

The death of any relative is an extremely difficult and emotional time. The death of a parent during the course of divorce proceedings which have not concluded can be particularly emotional for the children of the marriage. It can also be an extremely emotional time for the surviving spouse. The involvement of a family consultant at such stage is something to which serious consideration should be given.

The lawyer acting for the deceased spouse will have their retainer terminated at the point of death. It likely that they will be remunerated for any further work undertaken which is something to be borne carefully in mind. Questions may be raised by the children of the marriage who have an expectation of inheritance or simply a desire to understand exactly what the position is. This may be information which you are prepared to supply on a 'pro bono' basis.

The most important consideration when dealing with the 'silver separators' is to be conscious of the fact that the death of either party is a possibility and to ensure that adequate steps are taken at the commencement of divorce proceedings to ensure that unexpected consequences do not arise as a result of untimely death.

CHAPTER SIX
INCOME ISSUES IN LATER LIFE

The source of income through retirement years is an important consideration in later life in any event. It was only by 2018 that all employers had to automatically enrol their eligible workers into a workplace pension. The automatic enrolment process started in 2012 with the largest companies. Where only one of a couple might be working (which is more usually the case in the older generation), or where a reliance had been placed on downsizing the family home to provide for additional income in retirement the level of pension provision may veer towards the inadequate. This can be a particular problem for couples in retirement, particularly as life expectancy increases. Where a couple separate and find themselves having to run separate homes from the same income base the position can be quite dire.

When advising a client who is already passed retirement age or close to it, careful consideration needs to be given to that which has been put in place historically to meet the income requirements of the couple in retirement.

The starting point is to look at the pension provision. Might there be the possibility to 'top up' state pension contributions for one of the couple? This is an important point and is often overlooked. At the other end of the spectrum, has the threshold for lifetime pension contributions been exceeded thereby giving rise to taxation. The allowance for 2020 – 2021 is £1,073,100 (state pension being excluded).

Consideration may be given as to whether tax free lump sums can be drawn from any available pension provision in order to maximise immediate capital. The impact which this will have on income however must be considered carefully.

This is undoubtedly an area where an independent financial advisor may be of significant benefit. Calculations can be undertaken to evaluate the level of income which might be provided by the available income generating resources to take the couple to the end of their actuarially calculated lifespan. Budgets may need to be adjusted significantly.

It is not unusual for one of the couple to seek to retain the family home. If pension provision is significant and the party who hopes to retain their pension is able to move to alternative accommodation perhaps provided by a new partner this can seem initially attractive. The ability to continue to fund such level of accommodation may however be entirely out of reach. If pension is foregone in favour of the retention of a property for sentimental or other non-pragmatic reasons the source of income is immediately eradicated.

Whilst maintenance may be provided for a short period of time pending retirement, in a situation where capital resources including pension provision are to be divided equally (or fairly) between the separating couple it may not be reasonable for income provision to extend beyond the age of retirement.

Where income is insufficient however and in circumstances where individuals are regularly continuing in gainful employment past the state retirement age, is it reasonable for one spouse (perhaps who has historically not worked) to continue to claim income against a former spouse who chooses to work notwithstanding the fact that they have gone past the age of retirement?

The situation may be compounded in circumstances where one spouse intends to cohabit or remarry with a new (perhaps younger) partner who has a significant income of their own. There is of course no obligation on a subsequent spouse or partner to financially support the former spouse from the previous relationship. Inevitably however the spouse who has found a new partner will enjoy a far higher standard of living than their former spouse who is reliant on the assets of the marriage for financial support. Could this be a reason for a departure from equality? Presumably not as both of the couple may have the opportunity to meet new partners in the future and circumstances could change. Capital alteration to adjust for an income benefit provided by a new partner is unlikely to be seen as reasonable.

Pausing to consider the emotional repercussions, the spouse who did not want the divorce, perhaps whose husband/wife decided to end the marriage as a consequence of meeting a new partner, and who does not want to leave the family home will find it very difficult to come to terms with the significant financial changes which lie ahead of them. A necessity to downsize and conserve capital to create income will be a very bitter pill to swallow. If their spouse is able to maintain a far higher standard of living as a consequence of the new relationship which the other spouse views as the reason for the breakdown of the marriage and therefore necessarily their new disadvantaged circumstances, this will make the situation even harder to bear. A client who finds themselves in this situation will require additional support. The provision of a team to include a family consultant to support from the emotional perspective and a financial advisor to assist with the pragmatic discussion in relation to future budget and long-term financial planning becomes even more essential and valuable.

The situation also cross refers to the provision of financial support for adult children. As a combined unit, the parents may have been in a position to offer financial support for the provision of a house deposit or the payment of university fees. The separated parents may no longer be in a financial position to do so. The recovery of funds already passed to adult children would be problematic but the adherence to a promise made to younger children becomes difficult or impossible to fulfil. As already explained, this has an adverse effect upon the family dynamic.

A reduction in standard of living can be difficult to bear. Section 25 of the Matrimonial Causes Act 1973 suggest that standard of living is a relevant factor for consideration. Erroneously, many clients believe this to mean that an historic standard of living must be preserved. Unfortunately this is far from the case. It simply means that the financial bracket in which the couple find themselves whilst married will determine the sort of standard of living which would be reasonable moving forwards. Inevitably, where two households must be supported from the same resources the overall standard of living of each (unless supported by a third party) will reduce. Such situation can add to resentment and have a major impact on the family as a whole.

Affluent adult children may step forward to support their perceived disadvantaged parent. This can be unattractive and unhealthy and add to further family difficulties. Again the involvement of a family consultant can be beneficial in order to manage expectations and look at the bigger picture.

A clean break is of course not an inevitability albeit that it is something which in each case the Court "must" consider. In cases where parties are separating prior to retirement and where income is and continues to be high with no suggestion that the spouse in gainful employment will cease work at any designated point in the future, a joint lives maintenance order is still not out of the question. This may of course be a very long marriage and ongoing income may be a clear entitlement. In such a situation it is important to consider how income might be replaced in the event of the death of the paying party. Is some form of insurance in place? Is a reliance on the Inheritance (Provision for Family and Dependants) Act 1975 sufficient? Is there is a risk that the former spouse might pass their capital to a new spousal partner during their lifetime rendering an Inheritance Act claim entirely impotent?

In these circumstances the lawyer may wish to encourage their client to make provision for this eventuality if possible.

Rather than a joint lives maintenance order there may be a form of financial provision which provides for living expenses but also an additional sum with an expectation that this would be saved to provide a capital investment provision to assist with income in later life. In these circumstances a clean break at a designated point in the future (perhaps when the spouse in gainful employment ceases to be so) would be likely.

The provision of income to the end of the couple's respective lives is likely to be the most difficult area for resolution. The couple are likely to be of the generation where provision for retirement has not been as diligent as it may have been. The standard of living enjoyed whilst either or both of the couple were in gainful employment may have been high and accommodation may have been substantial. A reduction in status as a consequence of divided resources can also have a significant emotional effect and will need to be managed. The particular points to bear in mind are:-

- Ascertain at an early stage the resources available to provide for income in retirement.

- Involve an IFA at an early stage to deal with long term financial planning.

- A family consultant may be able to assist with the emotional difficulties faced where standard of living is compulsory reduced.

CHAPTER SEVEN
THE IMPACT OF THE NEW PARTNER

Either party to the marriage may have or become involved with a new partner. This will inevitably have an impact.

Where a couple separate in later life it is not unusual for one of the couple to have met a new partner. This may be the catalyst to bring an already ailing marriage to an end. The spouse who perceives themselves to have been abandoned is unlikely to have viewed the marriage as 'ailing' in the first instance but may have been entirely accepting of what perhaps was a compromised situation. They may have been prepared to accept the inadequacies and idiosyncrasies of married life because overall they found their lifestyle acceptable.

Rightly or wrongly the new partner will be perceived to be the cause of the breakdown of the marriage. Children will find themselves taking sides. Forming a tolerable relationship with the new partner of one parent may be seen as an act of disloyalty to the other. A demonstration of hostility towards the new partner of a parent may anger that parent. Whichever way round, disharmony is likely.

The management of the family dynamic can be extremely important if a relatively expeditious and cost-effective resolution of financial matters is to be achieved. In later life where time is inevitably relevant there may be a lack of desire, certainly on one side, to engage in protracted litigation. The involvement of a family consultant can therefore be invaluable.

The new partner may have children of their own. If one of the couple moves in with a new partner who has dependent children they may find themselves becoming financially responsible for the needs of those children which may be inadequately provided for by their own natural parent.

The imposition of a stepfamily brings its own problems. Loyalties inevitably become divided.

Where families are combined a question mark is raised over where the obligation lies to fund future accommodation. The new partner may be impecunious and unable to contribute towards the cost of accommodation.

If it is clear at an early stage that your client wishes to leave the marriage because they have entered into a new relationship it may well be that their spouse is not yet aware of that fact. An attempt to conceal that relationship is likely to be a hostage to a fortune. If the client believes the relationship to be long term the sooner it is disclosed to the other side the better. Often the client may believe that the introduction of a new partner (particularly a new partner who has a relatively high level of income) will adversely affect their financial claims against the resources of the marriage. This is of course not true. The new partner's obligation is only to meet their own living expenses in a confined houseful. They certainly have no obligation to fund or financially provide for their new partner's former spouse.

There is therefore absolutely no reason to hide a new relationship. A disingenuous approach can only have an adverse effect. Whilst upfront honesty may bring short term retribution it is without doubt the best way forwards.

CHAPTER EIGHT
IN PRACTICE

When a couple of this generation separate it is usually the decision of one while the world of the other suddenly and devastatingly falls apart. Rarely do the couple form the view that they have reached the end of a very long road and it is time for them to go their different ways.

If you are acting for the protagonist they will no doubt have given their situation very careful consideration but once having reached a decision they will want it to be implemented quickly so they can move on. Not infrequently they will have met a new partner. They may feel that time is not on their side.

One of the first steps which their lawyer will have to take is to manage expectations. The client may have formed their own view of how financial matters should be resolved and see your job as to sort everything out as quickly as possible. One could not be criticised for being surprised by the way in which someone who has been married for a long time can just want to move on with their life in a different direction and find it difficult to understand why their life partner for four or more decades does not simply acquiesce.

It is important not to forget that this is a marriage which may have started for all the wrong reasons when the couple were very young. The couple may have been operating on parallel lines for some time having unconsciously accepted compromise. That does not prevent one of the couple not to want any form of change.

Your client may have made a huge decision in their eyes bit having made it they just want to move on. They may tell you in the first instance that there is no 3rd party involved as they prefer to sort financial matters out before adding that ingredient to the mix. They may also incorrectly suspect that a new partner may have an adverse effect for them on any financial settlement. As their lawyer you will need to balance a sensitivity to the feelings of their spouse against the driven need on the part of your client to achieve a swift conclusion.

You may invite the other side to issue divorce proceedings but if they do you will want them to get on with it. You will want an undertaking to progress matters in timely fashion. Don't be afraid to issue divorce proceedings on the part of your client if the other side drag their feet. Either it may encourage the other party to issue proceedings because they know that if they don't you will, or if not at least you know that you are in control of the process.

If the party who wishes the marriage to end has a new partner they may consider that to petition on the grounds of the alleged unreasonable behaviour of the other is deeply unattractive. If however they want reasonably prompt finality it may be a sensitivity which they have to overcome. The obvious course of action for their spouse to take is 'do nothing'. A house cannot be sold without agreement or a court order. If the spouse doesn't want the marriage to end they have nothing to lose by just sitting tight and hoping that the other might change their mind. They may have allies in the form of the children who might seek to persuade.

If the protagonist just wants to get on with things the issue of proceedings will concentrate the mind. No claim for costs against the other side might be a dignified and generous gesture. The recipient may suggest issuing their own petition which may be an acceptable way forward. If they decide to defend, whilst that may cause delay and unnecessary cost, hopefully a decree of divorce would still ultimately be achieved.

Alongside the issue of proceedings it may also be prudent to issue an application in Form A. When doing so you may wish to reassure the other side that this is not intended to be seen as a provocative step but purely to set a time frame and that the hope is that matters can be resolved out of court.

If your client is the party who does not want the marriage to be over there will be different considerations to take into account. As already suggested, doing nothing will always be attractive. An additional consideration however is that initially the spouse who seeks the dissolution of the marriage will feel guilty which may translate into a more generous financial outcome. That feeling of guilt will quickly evaporate though. This might be a reason to just get on with things.

An emotionally distraught client will not be in the best of places for giving instructions and therefore progressing expeditiously may not be an option – irrespective of possible financial gain. You may want to suggest the involvement of a family coach/consultant at an early stage as your client will need support. Be wary of misguided support – especially from adult children however loyal they may appear to be – they will be going through their own trauma.

Your client may not have lived on their own for many years, if at all as they may have gong to marriage direct from their parents' home. They may never have had to manage their own finances. They will be frightened and require a great deal of reassurance. If their partner is determined to move forwards at a pace they may feel overwhelmed and insecure. You may want to try to steer the process towards a lawyer supported out of court method of resolution such as hybrid mediation in order to slow the process down and help your client settle and readjust while they make life decisions with advice.

Particularly if they have found a new partner, the spouse who is keen to bring the marriage to an end may initially feel guilty as a consequence of the apparent acute distress which their decision has inflicted upon the person with whom they have probably spent most of their adult life. Their desire to bring the process to an end as swiftly as possible may inspire generosity in the negotiation process. This may be something upon which to capitalise, not least because it is unlikely to last.

What the lawyer of the more reluctant spouse cannot do however is try to push or encourage their client towards a settlement. They may have a client who is just not in the right place to make lifetime decisions of this magnitude. The client may ask their lawyer to tell them what they should do. As a lawyer you give advice and 'reality test' options but you do not make choices on your client's behalf. The client needs to be in the right place to give instructions which can then be implemented.

The support of a family consultant may be invaluable. It is important to normalise this suggestion as no-one likes to feel that they are unusual in requiring professional emotional help. Make sure you have a list of family consultants readily available to provide which also helps to underline that this is a regular form of recommendation.

While the client works on their own emotional wellbeing it may be in their best interests to 'pause' the process. This may be directly opposed to the agenda of the protagonist who just wants to move on to their new way of life as quickly as possible. This is exactly the situation where divorce proceedings, probably on the basis of 'unreasonable behaviour' might be issued. Working alongside a family consultant you will need to evaluate whether your client needs time and how that can best be achieved. There may be no alternative other than to issue an Answer in reply to the Petition confirming that the proceedings are to be defended while the client gathers themselves together. The action taken by the other side may be the catalyst which makes your client recognise that they need to be in control rather than reacting to the steps taken by their spouse. The suggestion might be made that your client will issue their own petition for divorce rather than respond to the draft petition which has been provided.

Here the importance of provision of a draft petition in advance of issue is underlined, failing which costs may be wasted with the risk of both of the couple incurring a petition fee. If agreeing to the transfer of the role of Petitioner to the more reluctant spouse, it may be important for the other side to obtain an undertaking that the suit is progressed promptly.

Your client who wishes principally to maintain the status quo may instruct you to do whatever it takes to cause delay and in particular to avoid a sale of the family home for as long as possible. At the outset it is important to make clear the costs which may be incurred when adopting this strategy which will almost certainly result in litigation.

A property sale cannot be achieved without the consent of both parties or an order of the court. If the property is in the sole name of one of the couple a caution should be lodged with the land registry to uphold rights of occupation. Bear in mind that this is only effective until pronouncement of Decree Absolute.

The spouse who wants to get on with things will – as stated above – be likely to issue a Form A and must first attend a Mediation Information and Assessment meeting (MIAM) with an accredited mediator. The mediator must write to the other party inviting them to attend a similar meeting. Your client may wish to acquiesce to this request as participation in the mediation process may delay the issue of Form A and therefore any ultimate order for sale. You can see that an attempt could be made to drag this out for as long as possible with appointments being cancelled and re-arranged coupled with no real desire to sort things out. Costs will increase but your client might consider the expense to be worth it. It must be made clear to them that delay does not cause the inevitable to go away and that ultimately their increasingly impatient spouse will take steps to bring matters to a head.

What this dilatory approach may achieve however is a realisation by the other side that resolution is going to be neither quick nor easy and they may begin to look at imaginative solutions which give the other party something which the court might not provide, i.e. and offer which is too good to refuse and to which careful consideration is to be given. It may even be time limited (although I am not a fan of deadlines unless you have a clear plan of what you propose to do when the deadline has expired).

The emotional elements of the case are once again such an integral part of the negotiation process. A clear understanding of your client's objectives (which may change during the process) and what is motivating them is essential. The need to explore the costs incurred as a consequence of the adoption of any course of action, especially where costs might arguably be incurred unnecessarily, is also so vitally important.

CHAPTER NINE
OUT OF COURT OPTIONS

A clear understanding of the 'out of court' options available to a separating couple is an essential requirement for any family practitioner. The Family Law Court has been in difficulty for many years and the impact of COVID-19 has been severe. Whilst the desire of one party to do nothing other than cause delay can give rise to the only option for the other being an application to court, proper consideration should always be given to the alternatives. With the full support of the President of the Family Division, 'out of court' dispute resolution is poised to become the 'new normal',

I set out the most common forms of alternatives to court and when they might be used.

A. Early Neutral Evaluation

The couple may want an early 'steer' in relation to specific disputed issues or their circumstances generally. An early neutral evaluation would be undertaken by a solicitor, Barrister, or arbitrator jointly instructed by the couple either in person or through their legal advisors. This is not advice. It is purely a general overview of the case from someone who is not taking 'sides'. Neutral evaluation at an early stage can provide clarity for the couple before they become positional and incur unnecessary cost.

B. Mediation

Due to the government requirement to attend a Mediation Information and Assessment Meeting (MIAM) prior to the issue court proceedings, mediation is the form of 'out of court' practice best known to the public.

The mediator is a jointly instructed facilitator. Following safeguarding checks and, in financial cases, full financial disclosure, their role is to assist the couple in reaching their own outcome. The mediator will negate any power imbalance between the couple and will explore a variety of options with them. If they feel that independent advice is needed by either or both of the couple they will flag this up and the process will pause while advice is obtained.

Mediation can take place face to face or in separate rooms. In some cases solicitors may be present to provide support and immediate advice alongside the process. This is particularly the case in the form of mediation called **hybrid mediation**, provided by specially trained mediators.

Hybrid mediation is a cross between the family and civil mediation models. Lawyers will be directly involved in the process if instructed by the couple and may attend some or all of the meetings if required. The mediator may hold confidences (other than financial or where risk of harm is an issue) with each of the couple to assist the mediator in the negotiation process. Hybrid mediation is particularly useful in cases where conflict is high. It would be one of my preferred forms of dispute resolution for the 'silver separators' for a number of reasons:-

- Particularly where at least one of the parties is finding the process very difficult or is feeling very emotional and uncertain about the situation, the support of their lawyer within the process can be invaluable.

- Where appropriate, other relevant individuals can, by agreement, participate in the process which can be a helpful outlet for adult children.

- The structured approach can promote a feeling of security.

In mediation, although the couple may alight on a set of proposals with which they are happy to move forwards, this will not become a binding agreement until they have had the chance to take independent legal advice, thereby providing a second 'check' for the suggested outcome, which must be within the bracket of what a judge would order.

Ideally mediation will achieve resolution of all issues. If some points remain outstanding, arbitration, rather than court, may be the most time and cost-efficient means of adjudication.

C. Arbitration

If the couple cannot agree, an arbitrator can be jointly instructed to make a decision over all or just some of the outstanding issues. The arbitrator will be paid by the couple but because the process is so much quicker and more bespoke than the court service the overall cost (financially and emotionally) will be significantly less. Benefits include:-

- Choice of arbitrator

- Choice of date and location

- The arbitrator is available to make interim decisions 'on paper'
- Suitable for litigates in person as well as those with legal representation
- A private arbitrator is paid to achieve a fair and considered outcome

The IFLA (Institute of Family Law Arbitrators) website provides a list of trained arbitrators and is an excellent resource, providing access to the IFLA rules and all of the required forms.

D. Private FDR

Most cases settle at or shortly after the FDR stage following an indication from a judge who has heard the issues but not the evidence. This can be replicated on a private basis at any stage (if necessary more than once) to help guide the couple to a settlement. Choice of date and location again assist convenience.

The principal difference between the court and private FDR is that on a private basis you have someone dedicated only to your case for as long as you might require their assistance, often all day, at a shared fixed cost.

When selecting your private FDR judge a good start would be the IFLA website as trained arbitrators have the necessary skill set to conduct a private FDR.

E. The Certainty Project

This is a new way of working but using the tested court alternatives of mediation and arbitration, providing the couple with certainty of process duration and cost. An arbitrator is appointed jointly by the lawyers at the outset to have overall control of the case. The lawyers provide initial advice (you may even want to consider neutral evaluation at this stage if deemed helpful) and also deal with disclosure.

The couple will then move to mediation and the mediator will facilitate discussion. This can be via the hybrid process, which, as I have indicated earlier, is particularly suited to the 'silver separators'. If all issues are resolved the arbitrator delivers an award (finances) or determination (children) which the lawyers will turn into an order by consent.

If issues are unresolved the arbitrator will adjudicate those unresolved issues or the whole case if no progress has been made in mediation. The process will be completed within about six months which is parallel to the time required to achieve a divorce.

Costs are limited by the point at which resolution is achieved.

As a consequence of the certainty of time this process may not suit the client who wants to create as much delay as possible. Their lawyer may however want to discuss with them what that delay might realistically achieve and the downside of using less efficient and far more costly methods of resolution, such as court.

F. Collaborative Practice

Very popular in the first decade of this century, collaborative practice has been less prevalent recently. This is principally due to the fact that if the process breaks down each of the couple has to instruct a new lawyer from a different firm. Having taken the difficult first step to take legal advice, a client is not keen to be told that they might have to start all over again and find someone else to handle matters on their behalf. For this reason it may not be the most suitable method of dispute resolution for the 'silver separators'. That said, the approach of working together as a group of four (the couple and their respective lawyers), having the ability to bring others into the process such as an IFA of accountant or even a mediator, makes it a very safe and supported method of working. With the difficulties experienced within the court system this may once again become a good choice.

The couple and their lawyers will sign a participation agreement confirming that they will work together to resolve all issues by agreement, excluding the possibility of a court application. They will do so remotely or via face to face meetings and both lawyers will give their advice openly in front of the couple making everything very clear and transparent.

Whether you client is impatient for matters to be resolved quickly or keen to create as much delay as possible in order to perhaps keen the home or maintain the status quo for as long as they can, consideration should always be given to out of court options and those options should be explained fully to ensure that instructions are given from an informed position. If you feel that your client is not in the right place emotionally to make those decisions look at therapeutic support to help them reach that place before any decisions are made.

CHAPTER TEN
CASE STUDY

Ray is 64 and is married to Rosemary who is 65. They married 41 years ago and have three children, David age 38, Katie age 36 and William age 28. Ray is an accountant and is a partner in a small firm. Rosemary worked briefly as a secretary before David was born but has not worked since.

David is married to Joanna. They have two children, Sam and Mollie. Katie lives with her partner, Sophie. William still lives at home. Ray and Rosemary gave David and Katie £30k each towards their respective house purchases. They did not register their interest in the properties purchased.

Rosemary looks after David's children two mornings per week to help out with childcare costs as Joanna has returned to work part time.

Katie's relationship with Sophie is in difficulty and there is the possibility that they may separate. Their house is in joint names. Sophie has the higher income and wants to buy Katie out of the property but they is an issue over the status of the sum of £30k which Ray and Rosemary invested.

Ray and Rosemary's home is worth £900k and is mortgage free. They have lived there for the last 30 years. They have savings of about £200k which derive mainly from Ray's investments on the stock market. They have an ISA each worth £20k. Ray has a money purchase pension with a CETV of almost £1m. As a partner in the accountancy firm Ray has a 25% interest in the business premises. He will have to leave the partnership when he reaches the age of 67. He isn't keen to retire and has been discussing with a long-term good friend whether he could work with him on an 'in house' basis doing the accounts for him when he has retired from the partnership.

Ray has felt unhappy in the marriage for some time. He feels that Rosemary's interests lie with the children and grandchildren and that their own relationship has taken a back seat. He feels that David and Joanne take advantage of Rosemary. He also feels that William should be independent by now.

In contrast Rosemary is very happy with her life. She has a close circle of friends. She loves the fact that she spends so much time with her grandchildren and has a good relationship with all three children, especially William.

Ray has become increasingly keen on fitness. A friend of his recently died of a heart attack and Ray totally revised his diet and joined a local gym as a consequence. He suggested that Rosemary might join also, half knowing that she wouldn't want to. She didn't. Ray went to the gym three times a week after work and on Sunday mornings. It was there on a Sunday morning that Ray met Kellie, age 46, divorced with a 17 year-old daughter, Josie. Kellie works part time for a firm of local estate agents. Kellie belongs to a local cycling club; Ray joins too. Soon a relationship begins between them.

Ray believes that he has a chance of a new lease of life with Kellie. He thinks that Rosemary will be fine without him; after all she hardly seems to notice him when he is around. He doesn't want her to know about Kellie.

Ray decides he needs to take legal advice to see where he stands. Kellie suggests that he consult with the solicitor who handled her divorce but ray would prefer to find his own lawyer and arranges an appointment with Chris – a local family lawyer recommended by a colleague at work. He says that he is asking for his daughter Katie whose relationship is in difficulty.

Ray explains that his relationship with Rosemary is over. He wants to deal with everything fairly and to divorce on the new 'no fault' basis. He explains that he would expect Rosemary to have half of the value of the house and to keep her ISA. He thinks that she needs to get a job. He doesn't mention his relationship with Kellie. He hopes that everything can be resolved quickly.

Chris realises at an early stage that Ray has a number of misapprehensions. First, in relation to the decree proceeding, Chris explains that the 'no fault; ground is not yet actually available and could only be used if Ray and Rosemary are in agreement. Chris asks if either Ray or Rosemary has a new partner and receives a negative response. Chris goes on to explain that in that case the only ground for divorce would be 'unreasonable behaviour' or to separate and issue proceedings in two years' time provided Rosemary consents. Chris learns that Rosemary may not realise that the marriage has broken down from Ray's perspective. Chris recommends to Ray that he explain to Rosemary how he feels. Ray wants Chris to write to Rosemary telling her that the marriage is over. Chris prepares a draft letter explaining gently that Ray believes the marriage to be over and recommending that Rosemary consult with her own solicitor. Chris recommends that Ray speak to Rosemary before the letter arrives. Ray decides not to do so.

Chris has a client who has decided that he doesn't want to be married anymore and who wants things sorted out as quickly as possible. His expectations are unrealistic. Chris needs to manage those expectations and persuade Ray that his wife may need time to come to terms with his decision. In the initial meeting with Ray, Chris asks about Ray's family. Chris establishes the following:-

- *Rosemary has no idea how Rays feels about their marriage*
- *There is an adult child, William, still living at home on whom Ray's decision will impact hard*
- *Ray dos not understand that all assets held by either Ray, Rosemary or both are available for division between them*
- *Funds have been provided to two of the three children to help them purchase homes of their own. These funds were provided as a 'gift'.*

Chris prepares a draft letter and sends Ray a blank Form E to complete. Chris stresses to Ray the need for him to speak to Rosemary before the letter arrives. Ray discusses this with Kellie who agrees. Ray tells Kellie that he doesn't want to tell Rosemary or the children about their relationship until everything has been sorted out between himself and Rosemary.

That evening, after dinner, Ray realises that he needs to talk to Rosemary about the letter which will arrive from his solicitor in the morning. He has already moved some of his things into the spare bedroom unbeknown to her.

This is a marriage of more than 40 years duration and the couple have brought up three children yet this will be the first time Rosemary realises for certain that Ray intends to leave. Of course you might say that she should have known that something was wrong but she has been content with live as it was and thought that this would continue for the rest of her life. Her expectations for the future have been very different to Ray's. The shock will hit Rosemary hard.

Rosemary hears Ray's words but somehow they don't go in; she can't quite understand or believe what he seems to be trying to tell her.

Ray tells her that he has been unhappy for many years and that he expects she has too. He thinks it will be better for both of them if they separate and he tells her that he has moved into the spare bedroom.

Rosemary feels numb. She waits to receive the letter from Ray's solicitor which arrives by post the following morning. She has said nothing to William. She phones David. Fortunately she doesn't have the grandchildren that day – Ray planned it to be so. David phones his father to find out what is going on – full of mixed emotions. It is a conversation which Ray does not want to have and he is angered by the judgemental approach taken by his eldest child. David contacts his siblings. Katie isn't really surprised; William is incensed and angry with himself that he is still living in the same house but didn't see this coming.

All three children take the view that their father needs to come to his senses. They meet up after work to decide what to do. David has a recommendation of a good family law solicitor. He thinks that Rosemary needs to take legal advice to find out where she stands and that one of them should go with her. He puts himself forward to do so and the others agree. They think that perhaps Ray should not know at this stage that their mother will be taking advice. Katie is reluctant to take sides but is persuaded by her brothers that they must support their mother – with whom only David has had a conversation so far.

David accompanies William to the family home where they find their mother distraught. Ray has gone to the gym straight from work. David tells Rosemary that everything will be fine and that he is arranging an appointment for her to see a solicitor just to discuss where she stands. Rosemary doesn't want to do this. She wants to bury her head in the sand in the hope that Ray will change his mind. The boys persuade her that she must. Rosemary feels as though she is in a daze. The boys say that they will go with her and that she mustn't tell Ray. When Ray finally comes home he goes straight to the spare room without speaking to Rosemary.

The day comes when Rosemary is to see the solicitor – the first appointment having been cancelled because she didn't feel up to it. David and William go with her to meet Alex who has been recommended to David s a family law specialist. Alex is a solicitor but also a mediator. During the meeting David and to a lesser extent William try to speak for their mother who is clearly overwhelmed by everything which is going on around her. Alex skilfully engages with Rosemary, asking her questions about her circumstances and listening carefully to what she has to say. Alex suggests doing nothing at present but suggests a second meeting to discuss what Rosemary might expect financially were Ray insistent on bringing the marriage to an end. Alex provides Rosemary with the details of a family consultant who may be able to provide her with valuable, affordable emotional support.

Alex's professional obligations are to Rosemary but there is a need to balance the involvement of David and William who are attending the meeting to support their mother. Alex needs to understand the dynamic of this family and so needs to spend time listening and gathering information. Alex recognises that to look at outcomes at this stage would be too much for Rosemary to take in and so recommends a family consultant for emotional support (someone professional and neutral to take over from her sons) and arranges another meeting to look at financial outcome in a 'worst case' scenario i.e. if Ray is determined to bring this long marriage to an end.

Rosemary has given the letter which she received from Ray's solicitor to Alex who will respond at this stage by simply confirming instruction by Rosemary, David and William resolve to say nothing to their father at this stage – something which William finds difficult as he is living under the same roof. A further appointment is made with Alex to consider Rosemary's position on divorce. In the meantime Chris writes to Alex inviting Rosemary to issue divorce proceedings but advising that Ray will do so if she chooses not to. A 14-day time window for response is given. Alex decides, not to send this to Rosemary, but to discuss with her at the forthcoming meeting.

Katie feels that she should attend this meeting with her mother and brothers too. Her relationship with Sophie has broken down and she was considering returning to live at home in the short term while she sorts her own life out. Alex is surprised when all three adult children arrive at the office. Rosemary says that she would like them to hear what Alex has to say.

Should Alex have asked that just one of the children sit in with Rosemary for the meeting and the others sit outside. Would the selection of one over the other two have been bad for this family dynamic or would this have been better than Alex trying to manage these three additional adults during the meeting?

David is furious to hear that his father is putting pressure on his mother to get on with a divorce and incredulous that Ray might issue a petition based upon Rosemary's alleged unreasonable behaviour. Alex takes Rosemary through the options re her marriage and takes her through what is likely to happen re the finances. David, Katie and William interject constantly and Alex sees that Rosemary is struggling to take anything in. Alex confirms that all advice will be provided in writing also. The meeting lasts for well over two hours. Alex is exhausted by the end. David suggests to the others that they take their mother for lunch as there is much to discuss. Alex feels that Rosemary appears rather overwhelmed and is allowing David to take charge.

Alex has to consider and advise Rosemary on the following issues:-

Decree proceedings

- *Rosemary could simply do nothing and see if Ray will actually issue proceedings. An 'unreasonable behaviour' petition is very subjective and most married couples can use this ground if they put their minds to this. Ray could also claim costs against Rosemary but may be unlikely to do so as he is the stronger financial party and is the one who wants the divorce. Alex could ask for more time for Rosemary to think about things as she has not had a proper chance to 'catch up' with the decisions that Ray has made in his own mind.*

- *Rosemary could agree to issue a petition which puts her in control of the process. Alex could slow the process down*

- *If Ray does issue a petition Rosemary could defend it and file an Answer. This will cause the proceedings to become defended and costs would increase but 'delay' would be achieved*

Alex suspects that Ray may have a new partner. Alex does not reveal this to Rosemary but suggests that if Ray can be persuaded to allow Rosemary more time to come to terms with the situation the decisions which she has to make may become easier.

Financial Remedies

- *Should Rosemary consider severing the joint tenancy on the family home?*

- *Does Rosemary need to 'top up' her state pension?*

- *How are the immediate financial arrangements working? Is Ray likely to change anything as Rosemary has no income of her own?*
- *What are the capital resources?*
- *The starting point for division is equality*
- *Rosemary does not need to provide a home for William and certainly not for Katie*
- *Ray and Rosemary intended to give William £30k for a deposit for a property. This may not be affordable or Ray may not agree to this*
- *What is the status of any money which Katie may receive from Sophie as a consequence of the £30k deposit provided by her parents when their property was purchased?*
- *Will there need to be a pension sharing report to properly calculate the pension share? Ray's CETV is close to the maximum lifetime allowance.*
- *What will Rosemary receive from Ray by way of financial support and for how long – especially if Ray continues to work beyond the age of 67?*
- *Might Rosemary be expected to look at some kind of gainful employment? She is providing childcare for David. Should she be paid to do this moving forwards?*

A 'lively' discussion breaks out between David, Katie and William over lunch with their mother.

How can it be fair, feels William, for David and Kate to have received £30k towards a house deposit but he might not?? Katie, it seems, will get the money back in cash from Sophie (who wants to do the 'decent' thing as he has met a new partner) but why should she keep that?? William needs to have space to work from home as a consequence of 'lockdown' or be close to a train station when he returns to work in the office in London yet it seems his requirements will be ignored???

David cannot believe that their mother could even think about finding some kind of job and is even more annoyed by the suggestion that he and Joanna might pay Rosemary to look after her own grandchildren.

Rosemary becomes increasingly distressed and overwhelmed. Katie is concerned that her brothers seem to be focussing on how this affects them rather than their mother. The boys feel that she would say that as she is the one about to walk away with £30k in cash. Katie makes the point that she doesn't have a home. Katie decides that she will talk to Ray to see if he is really serious about all this. He is hardly speaking to Rosemary now and is out of the house a lot. Rosemary had already asked William to keep out of his father's way at home and not to start any arguments. Deep down she hopes that Ray will change his mind if everything stays calm. Rosemary would prefer that no-one talked to ray at the moment but the three children agree that Katie might be best placed to do so and Rosemary reluctantly goes along with this. She remembers that Alex had provided her with the details of a family consultant and thinks she will make contact but decides not to tell the children. She wonders how all this advice is going to be paid for. She feels very scared and, despite the overt support from her children, very alone.

Katie arranges to meet with Ray away from the family home on the pretext that she needs to talk to him about the breakdown of her relationship with Sophie. Katie has always felt that Ray was secretly pleased that things had gone wrong. Her relationship with her father has recently been the best it has been for a long time so she hoped to capitalise on this and have a frank discussion.

When they meet, Ray explains that he has been unhappy for many years and that he and Rosemary have just co-existed for some time, not unhappy but not really happy either. He tells his daughter that he has reached a stage in life where he realises that life is a fragile thread and he wants to make the most of the time he has left. Katie asks if he has met someone else which he categorically denies. Katie remains suspicious. Ray makes it very clear that he will not change his mind. He reassures Katie that her mother will be fine and 'well provided for'. He makes it clear that whatever Katie receives from Sophie will be hers to keep. He asks Katie to try to persuade Rosemary to issue a divorce petition but stresses that he won't wait forever.

Katie reports back to her brothers. Rosemary meets with the Family Consultant. She decides to do nothing for the moment. Life at home is difficult. William is struggling to stay out of the situation at home and the atmosphere is tense.

Kellie asks Ray what is happening. Her child support and spousal maintenance will come to an end when Josie reaches 18 which is now only a few months away. She has had a couple of relationships which have gone nowhere but she sees Ray (who is older than her) as different and she wants to make this work. She doesn't want to put pressure on Ray and realises that their relationship is in its early stages. He has made it clear that he wants to get on with things and sounds serious. Kellie is considering asking to get Ray to agree to move in with her at a point in the future.

Kellie clearly has some financial motivation to make things work with Ray. Ray wants to get on with things. Rosemary's preference is to do nothing. The children are potentially volatile and unpredictable and focussing on self-interest.

Chris needs to balance Ray's desire to get on with things against the risk of divorce proceedings becoming contested and everything slowing down as a consequence. Chris suspects that Ray may have a new partner and will raise the question with him.

Alex needs to provide Rosemary with as much support as possible which has been done in part by the recommendation of a Family Consultant.

Alex also needs to be cognisant of the involvement of the three adult children and the effect which their views may have on instructions given.

A few weeks pass and nothing really happens. Kellie has asked Ray what is going on. Ray meets with Chris who explains his options again. Ray seems agitated and very keen to make progress. Chris asks if he has met someone. Ray says that he has made friends with a woman he has met at the gym but is unsure if it is serious. Chris explains that Rosemary may be prepared to issue an adultery petition if that is an available ground.

Ray is very unsure about this and thinks Kellie would not be happy with this suggestion. His relationship with Rosemary was, in his mind, over long before he met Kellie.

Rosemary now feels much stronger having spoken to the Family Consultant, Rebecca, with whom she feels she has developed a good relationship; she finds her easy to talk to. She has decided that she doesn't want to leave her home or change her life just because that is what Ray wants and she is going to hold her ground. She contacts Alex and gives instructions to simply do nothing.

Ray is finding the lack of progress exasperating. Life at home is terrible and he is spending most of his time somewhere else, usually now with Kellie who tentatively suggests that he might like to move in. Ray contacts Chris demanding an update.

If Ray wants to make progress he will have to take the initiative and issue divorce proceedings. He would be well advised to issue financial remedy proceedings at the same time, after attending a MIAM. There is no benefit to Rosemary to do anything but if she is compelled to complete paperwork and incur costs she may be forced to engage.

One of Rosemary's friends spots Ray in his car with Kellie. They seem very 'cosy'. The friend convinces herself that she must tell Rosemary – after all she would want to know. At first Rosemary is in disbelief but gradually she puts together in her mind little things that she has noticed. The credit card statements do not suggest that Ray has been eating out but he has not been eating at home. He never puts his mobile phone down anywhere. She is distraught. She receives a draft divorce petition from Ray's solicitor. She arranges another meeting with Alex and asks Katie to go with her. Katie feels awkward as she has, if anything, taken Ray's side. She agrees to go with her mother provided Rosemary does not tell her brothers of her suspicions. They tell Alex what Rosemary believes to be true. Alex suggests writing to Chris to say the draft petition is not agreed but Rosemary will petition on the basis of Ray's adultery with an unnamed person. She will also claim costs. Otherwise Ray's petition, if issued, will be defended.

If Ray wants a divorce accepting an adultery petition would appear to be the easiest route. Kellie will be very unhappy and he doesn't want that. The alternatives are unattractive. Ray doesn't really want to issue a divorce petition and certainly doesn't want to be embroiled in a defended divorce. He has not told his business partners what has been going on, although they are aware that he is preoccupied.

It is clear to Alex that Ray will issue and it would be better for Rosemary if she were in control of the process. Rosemary may do better in the financial negotiations this way as Ray may feel guilty and also want things over with quickly. Although Rosemary still wants the process to be delayed as much as possible Alex feels better able to achieve this if Rosemary is the Petitioner. Alex can deal with things as slowly as possible – helped by the Court which is far from efficient.

Ray decides, reluctantly, after being reassured by Chris that Kellie will not be named in the proceedings and he will suffer in the financial proceedings as a consequence, to agree to Rosemary issuing an adultery petition.

Chris needs to ensure that Rosemary gives an undertaking to deal with the proceedings promptly to the decree nisi stage. As Ray wants to maintain momentum he should issue Form A as soon as he has been served with the divorce papers, thereby regaining control. Alex may want to consider advising Rosemary to issue Form A with her divorce papers to maintain control. This may be more than Rosemary is prepared to do but the options need to be fully explained to her. It is always preferable to be the Applicant in contested financial proceedings and just because proceedings are issued doesn't mean they can't be adjourned to follow an out of court alternative. The new process – The Certainty Project – which offers the combination of mediation and arbitration with an arbitrator having overarching control of the process throughout, is an extremely time and cost efficient means of resolution – providing Ray with the certainty of time frame but Rosemary with the continuity of adjudicator alongside the option to try to agree matter with Ray. Although Rosemary might feel very nervous about mediating with Ray, the hybrid mediation option which offers separate meeting with the mediator and the opportunity to have your lawyer with you throughout the process if required might work well. If all issues can be resolved then a consent order can be produced. If some issues simply can't be agreed the arbitrator can make an adjudication over just that which is outstanding.

Chris and Alex each need to demonstrate considerable skill to encourage their clients forwards in the knowledge that they each have significant emotional issues to deal with. Might Ray also benefit from the input of a Family Consultant?

What happens next?

- David and William discover that their father is having an affair and are furious. The situation at the family home becomes so untenable that Ray moves out. He initially stays with relative but eventually moves in with Kellie. This potentially impacts on the maintenance which she receives from her former husband.

- Ray pays a fixed amount into the joint account to cover the running costs of the family home and opens an account in his sole name into which his drawings are paid. He tells William that he must pay rent to live at home and David that he must pay Rosemary for looking after the children. Both sons are now livid. Rosemary tells them she won't take money from either of them. Katie can see both sides and decides not to get involved. William believes that Katie should pay back the £30k for the house deposit when she receives it from Sophie and that he should have the same money as his siblings. He sees his father as supporting Kellie's daughter rather than him. Rosemary is very worried about him.

- David and William try to persuade their mother to bring an application for interim financial support as they both feel that their father is not properly supporting her. Rosemary doesn't know what she should do. Alex warns her that an interim application is viewed on a very 'broad brush' basis. Rosemary has an ISA in her name to supplement and there is a risk that a court would expect William to pay something to live at home and David to pay for childcare. Rosemary decided not to proceed. The relationship between father and his two sons deteriorates still further.

- Either Ray or Rosemary could issue a Form A. If Rosemary wants to stay in the house for as long as possible she may want to do everything she can to cause delay. Ray may decide to issue in case Rosemary is un co-operative but may suggest mediation to run alongside. Hybrid mediation would probably suit Rosemary the best as she can be supported within the process by Alex

- The Certainty Project is an option to consider. Intended to provide certainty of personnel, timing and cost, the project could be the perfect process for Ray and Rosemary. An arbitrator would be selected to provide overarching control of the process. Disclosure would be dealt with by Chris and Alex (the solicitors) with questions raised and answered. The couple would then move to mediation, probably hybrid mediation, supported by their lawyers in separate meetings. If agreement is reached an Award by consent would be delivered by the arbitrator. If some or all issues remain outstanding, the arbitrator will adjudicate and provide an Award which the solicitors will turn into an order by consent. The whole process will last six months.

- A pension sharing report will be required, not least due to the ages of the parties and the value of Ray's pension fund. Joint instruction should be provided as soon as possible as a pension report could take up to 6 months to be available.

- A pension sharing order will be made to provide equality of income in retirement or value. Where the couple are older the equalising of income is likely.

- The starting point for division of capital is equality. Whether Ray can live in Kellie's home is not relevant but if Ray has a mortgage capacity might Rosemary receive a slightly larger capital share?

- Pre pension income may be the biggest problem. If the pension share if drawn immediately meets Rosemary's income needs could there be a clean break? Should Ray pay maintenance to Rosemary in the short term. Could this be capitalised?

- Both Rosemary and Ray need to make new Wills. The fact that Ray has new dependents is something that David, William and perhaps Katie may struggle with.

- What steps can this family take to remedy the rifts between Ray and particularly his sons? Can the Family Consultant help with this? Perhaps the damage caused cannot be rectified? What long term effect might this have on the children?

CHAPTER ELEVEN
CONCLUSION

Representing a client who is separating in the later years of their life brings very particular challenges. There is a much wider picture to be cognisant of than just the requirements of the couple. Anticipation of influencing factors is so important as is listening and asking the right questions. An understanding of the likely approach taken by the other side is vital to achieve a balance of desired outcome and the management of expectations.

Minor children are the first consideration for separating couples but adult children, who from the point of view of the court are not relevant, are more likely to be adversely impacted by the separation of their parents. Their influence on the process can be significant.

This age group now form the largest within the divorce process. Make sure you are equipped to provide them and their wider family with the advice, care and support that they need.

MORE BOOKS BY LAW BRIEF PUBLISHING

A selection of our other titles available now:-

'Covid-19, Homeworking and the Law – The Essential Guide to Employment and GDPR Issues' by Forbes Solicitors
'Covid-19, Force Majeure and Frustration of Contracts – The Essential Guide' by Keith Markham
'Covid-19 and Criminal Law – The Essential Guide' by Ramya Nagesh
'Covid-19 and Family Law in England and Wales – The Essential Guide' by Safda Mahmood
'Covid-19 and the Implications for Planning Law – The Essential Guide' by Bob Mc Geady & Meyric Lewis
'Covid-19, Residential Property, Equity Release and Enfranchisement – The Essential Guide' by Paul Sams and Louise Uphill
'Covid-19, Brexit and the Law of Commercial Leases – The Essential Guide' by Mark Shelton
'Covid-19 and the Law Relating to Food in the UK and Republic of Ireland – The Essential Guide' by Ian Thomas
'A Practical Guide to the General Data Protection Regulation (GDPR) – 2nd Edition' by Keith Markham
'Ellis on Credit Hire – Sixth Edition' by Aidan Ellis & Tim Kevan
'A Practical Guide to Working with Litigants in Person and McKenzie Friends in Family Cases' by Stuart Barlow
'Protecting Unregistered Brands: A Practical Guide to the Law of Passing Off' by Lorna Brazell
'A Practical Guide to Secondary Liability and Joint Enterprise Post-Jogee' by Joanne Cecil & James Mehigan

'A Practical Guide to the Pre-Action RTA Claims Protocol for Personal Injury Lawyers' by Antonia Ford
'A Practical Guide to Neighbour Disputes and the Law' by Alexander Walsh
'A Practical Guide to Forfeiture of Leases' by Mark Shelton
'A Practical Guide to Coercive Control for Legal Practitioners and Victims' by Rachel Horman
'A Practical Guide to Rights Over Airspace and Subsoil' by Daniel Gatty
'Tackling Disclosure in the Criminal Courts – A Practitioner's Guide' by Narita Bahra QC & Don Ramble
'A Practical Guide to the Law of Driverless Cars – Second Edition' by Alex Glassbrook, Emma Northey & Scarlett Milligan
'A Practical Guide to TOLATA Claims' by Greg Williams
'Artificial Intelligence – The Practical Legal Issues' by John Buyers
'A Practical Guide to the Law of Prescription in Scotland' by Andrew Foyle
'A Practical Guide to the Construction and Rectification of Wills and Trust Instruments' by Edward Hewitt
'A Practical Guide to the Law of Bullying and Harassment in the Workplace' by Philip Hyland
'How to Be a Freelance Solicitor: A Practical Guide to the SRA-Regulated Freelance Solicitor Model' by Paul Bennett
'A Practical Guide to Prison Injury Claims' by Malcolm Johnson
'A Practical Guide to the Small Claims Track' by Dominic Bright
'A Practical Guide to Advising Clients at the Police Station' by Colin Stephen McKeown-Beaumont
'A Practical Guide to Antisocial Behaviour Injunctions' by Iain Wightwick
'Practical Mediation: A Guide for Mediators, Advocates, Advisers, Lawyers, and Students in Civil, Commercial, Business, Property, Workplace, and Employment Cases' by Jonathan Dingle with John Sephton
'The Mini-Pupillage Workbook' by David Boyle

'A Practical Guide to Crofting Law' by Brian Inkster
'A Practical Guide to Spousal Maintenance' by Liz Cowell
'A Practical Guide to the Law of Domain Names and Cybersquatting' by Andrew Clemson
'A Practical Guide to the Law of Gender Pay Gap Reporting' by Harini Iyengar
'A Practical Guide to the Rights of Grandparents in Children Proceedings' by Stuart Barlow
'NHS Whistleblowing and the Law' by Joseph England
'Employment Law and the Gig Economy' by Nigel Mackay & Annie Powell
'A Practical Guide to Noise Induced Hearing Loss (NIHL) Claims' by Andrew Mckie, Ian Skeate, Gareth McAloon
'An Introduction to Beauty Negligence Claims – A Practical Guide for the Personal Injury Practitioner' by Greg Almond
'Intercompany Agreements for Transfer Pricing Compliance' by Paul Sutton
'Zen and the Art of Mediation' by Martin Plowman
'A Practical Guide to the SRA Principles, Individual and Law Firm Codes of Conduct 2019 – What Every Law Firm Needs to Know' by Paul Bennett
'A Practical Guide to Adoption for Family Lawyers' by Graham Pegg
'A Practical Guide to Industrial Disease Claims' by Andrew Mckie & Ian Skeate
'A Practical Guide to Redundancy' by Philip Hyland
'A Practical Guide to Vicarious Liability' by Mariel Irvine
'A Practical Guide to Applications for Landlord's Consent and Variation of Leases' by Mark Shelton
'A Practical Guide to Relief from Sanctions Post-Mitchell and Denton' by Peter Causton
'A Practical Guide to Equity Release for Advisors' by Paul Sams
'A Practical Guide to Unlawful Eviction and Harassment' by Stephanie Lovegrove
'A Practical Guide to the Law Relating to Food' by Ian Thomas

‘A Practical Guide to Financial Services Claims’ by Chris Hegarty
‘The Law of Houses in Multiple Occupation: A Practical Guide to HMO Proceedings’ by Julian Hunt
‘A Practical Guide to Unlawful Eviction and Harassment’ by Stephanie Lovegrove
‘A Practical Guide to Solicitor and Client Costs’ by Robin Dunne
‘Occupiers, Highways and Defective Premises Claims: A Practical Guide Post-Jackson – 2nd Edition’ by Andrew Mckie
‘A Practical Guide to Financial Ombudsman Service Claims’ by Adam Temple & Robert Scrivenor
'A Practical Guide to Advising Schools on Employment Law' by Jonathan Holden
‘A Practical Guide to Running Housing Disrepair and Cavity Wall Claims: 2nd Edition’ by Andrew Mckie & Ian Skeate
‘A Practical Guide to Holiday Sickness Claims – 2nd Edition’ by Andrew Mckie & Ian Skeate
‘Arguments and Tactics for Personal Injury and Clinical Negligence Claims’ by Dorian Williams
‘A Practical Guide to QOCS and Fundamental Dishonesty’ by James Bentley
‘A Practical Guide to Drone Law’ by Rufus Ballaster, Andrew Firman, Eleanor Clot
‘A Practical Guide to Compliance for Personal Injury Firms Working With Claims Management Companies’ by Paul Bennett
‘A Practical Guide to the Landlord and Tenant Act 1954: Commercial Tenancies’ by Richard Hayes & David Sawtell
‘A Practical Guide to Dog Law for Owners and Others’ by Andrea Pitt
‘RTA Allegations of Fraud in a Post-Jackson Era: The Handbook – 2nd Edition’ by Andrew Mckie
‘RTA Personal Injury Claims: A Practical Guide Post-Jackson’ by Andrew Mckie
‘On Experts: CPR35 for Lawyers and Experts’ by David Boyle
‘An Introduction to Personal Injury Law’ by David Boyle

'A Practical Guide to Chronic Pain Claims' by Pankaj Madan
'A Practical Guide to Claims Arising from Fatal Accidents' by James Patience
'A Practical Guide to Subtle Brain Injury Claims' by Pankaj Madan

These books and more are available to order online direct from the publisher at www.lawbriefpublishing.com, where you can also read free sample chapters. For any queries, contact us on 0844 587 2383 or mail@lawbriefpublishing.com.

Our books are also usually in stock at www.amazon.co.uk with free next day delivery for Prime members, and at good legal bookshops such as Wildy & Sons.

We are regularly launching new books in our series of practical day-to-day practitioners' guides. Visit our website and join our free newsletter to be kept informed and to receive special offers, free chapters, etc.

You can also follow us on Twitter at www.twitter.com/lawbriefpub.

www.ingramcontent.com/pod-product-compliance
Lightning Source LLC
LaVergne TN
LVHW022310200926
848481LV00004B/1265